RED
CRAB
I0791448

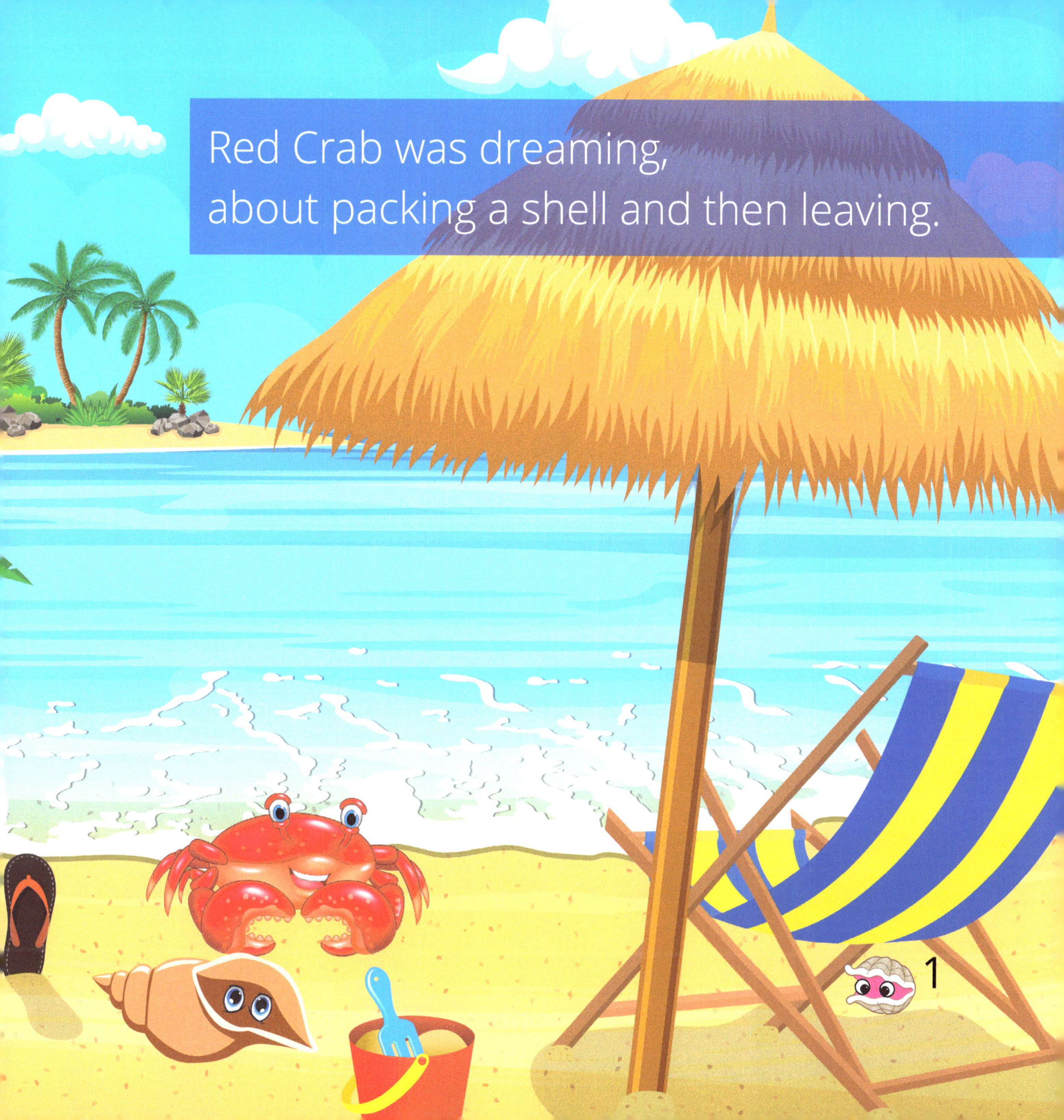

Red Crab was dreaming,
about packing a shell and then leaving.
1

But the ocean was fierce and ever so rough,
and Red Crab, well, he was not so tough.

2

He spotted a shell that he felt would do well,
which a hermit crab was hoping to sell.

FOR
SALE

3

"SOLD," Red Crab said on the shore,
"I can spare a dollar, but nothing more."
FOR SALE
100
4

5

Shortly after setting sail,
Red Crab approached a storm and gale.

6

Waves were tall in the raging squall,
and then they sank, Red Crab, and all.

To the ocean bed went the stricken boat,
not even Red Crab could stay afloat.

Feeling all alone but not for long,
fishes arrived to see what was wrong.

Just as Red Crab was about to speak,
the fishes vanished without a squeak.

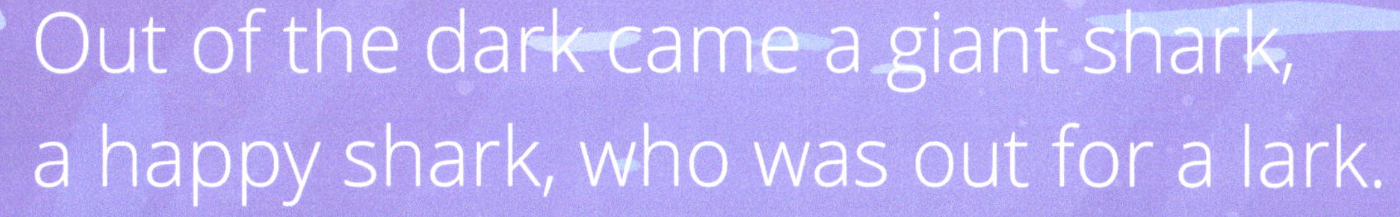

Out of the dark came a giant shark,
a happy shark, who was out for a lark.

11

"I'm going to New York to Central Park,"
said Red Crab to the giant shark.

They became surrounded by some jellyfish,
which turtles enjoy as a tasty dish.

The giant shark went on his way,
as a turtle and Red Crab, started to play.
14

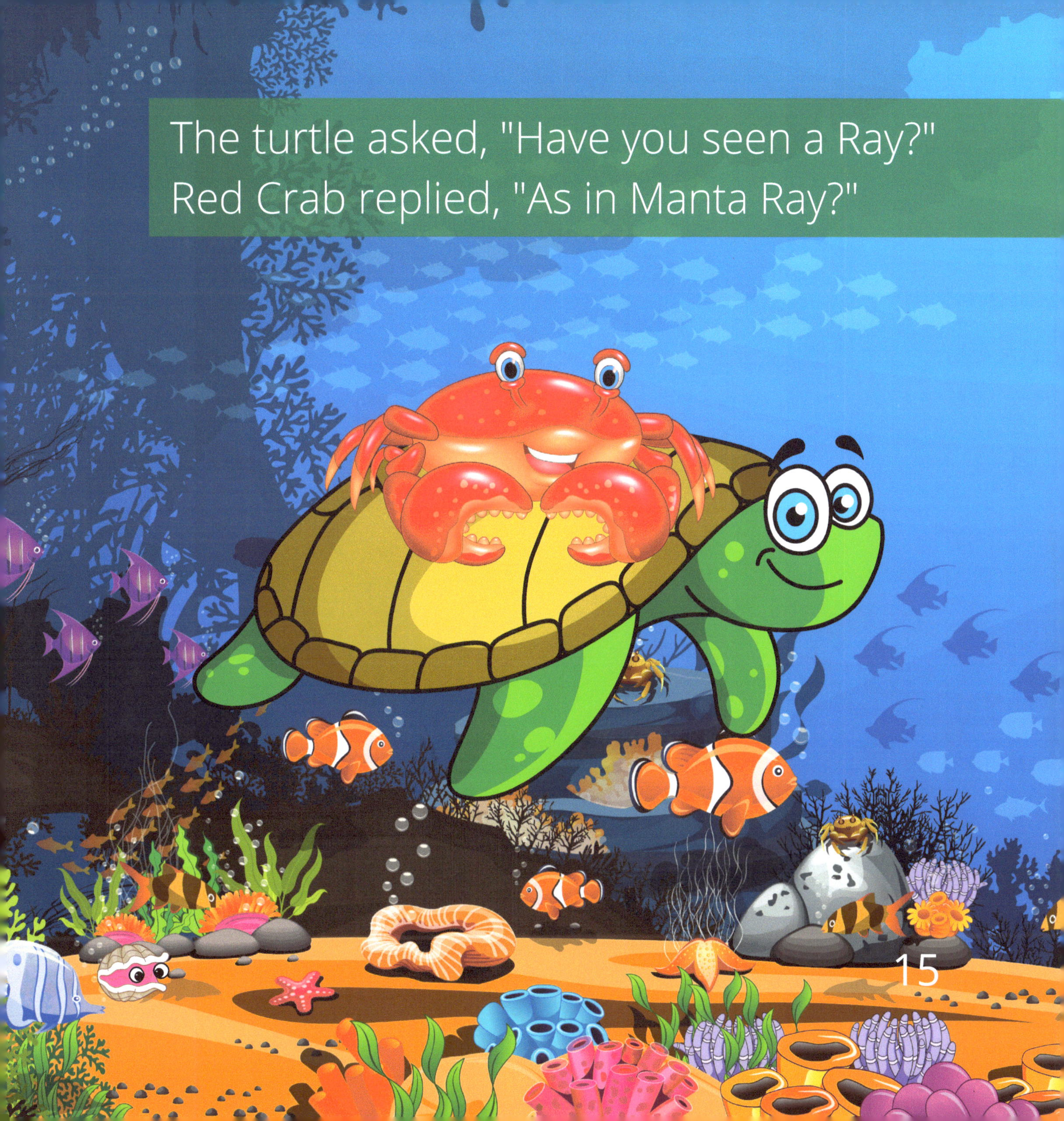
The turtle asked, "Have you seen a Ray?"
Red Crab replied, "As in Manta Ray?"

15

The turtle responded with, "Let's go see,"
as he knew of a place that there were three.

Manta Rays are massive and shy,
they glide in the water like birds in the sky.

Red Crab smiled to see a Manta Ray,
turtle smiled and bid Red Crab, good day.

Red Crab looked up and decided to rise,
he couldn't believe what he saw with his eyes.

Dolphins were splashing and playing games,
so Red Crab waved and asked their names.

"I'm Flipper, and there is Boto, Carly and Dab." "Hello, Flipper, my name is Red Crab."
21

They swam so fast the ocean vast,
and with a splash, they arrived at last.

22

To touch the sand, it felt so great,
but he had to move, or he would be late.

A giant crab stood proud and blue,
so then Red Crab, he stood proud too.

Red Crab was tired and needed to sleep,
so the giant blue crab said, "Take the jeep."

25

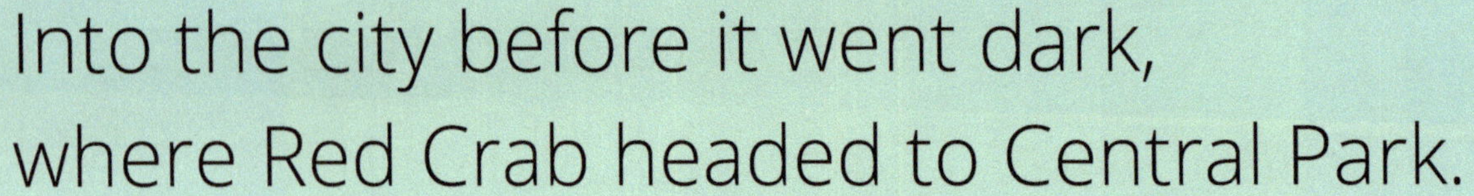

Into the city before it went dark,
where Red Crab headed to Central Park.

26

Arriving at the park at 8,
Red Crab wasn't alone,
he was with his best mate.

The clam was his friend,
her name was Claire.
Claire was by his side,
all the way there.

28

They sat on a bridge having fun and laughter,
and both Red Crab and Claire,
lived happily ever after.

Happy Red Crabs